# THE HISTORY, ART & IMAGERY OF
THE PFISTER HOTEL

THE HISTORY, ART & IMAGERY OF

THE PFISTER HOTEL

Thomas J. Jordan
Photography by Jay W. Filter

PUBLISHED BY THE MARCUS CORPORATION

Published by the Marcus Corporation.

100 E Wisconsin Avenue, #1950
Milwaukee, Wisconsin 53202
Phone: 414-905-1000
marcuscorp.com

© 2013 The Marcus Corporation. All rights reserved. No part of this publication may be reproduced or transmitted in any form or by any means, electronic or mechanical, including photocopy, recording, or any other information storage and retrieval system, or otherwise without written permission from the publisher.

Author: Thomas J. Jordan
Photographer: Jay W. Filter
Designer: Steve Biel
Typeset in Village and Gotham

Photo Credits:
Pages 24, 26, 27, 33, 42, 43, 51, 57, 73, 88, 89, 114, 115, 116, 117, 170, 224 vintage items courtesy of Milwaukee County Historical Society.
Pages 28-31 courtesy of Milwaukee Public Library
Pages 86, 98-99, 102, 113, 127, 128, 130-131 photographed by Cory Zimmermann, Z2 Marketing.
Page 88 barbershop images provided by Derek Dahlsad.
Page 272 provided by Harley-Davidson Museum
Page 274 provided by the Milwaukee Brewers Baseball Club
Page 276 provided by the Pabst Theater, C.J. Foeckler, photographer
Page 277 provided by the Marcus Center for the Performing Arts
Page 278 provided by the Summerfest/Milwaukee World Festival, Inc.

Various city images were secured with the assistance of Brook G. Smith, Tyler Barnes, Andy Nelson, Ann Birkinbine, Heidi Lofy, and Jessica Meilier. Sincere thanks to Mary Fisher, Tom Augustine and Michael C. Williams of United States District Court.
Vintage postcard (page 47) courtesy of www.uffduhhh.com

Thanks to the helpful staff of the Arts and Humanities desk at the Milwaukee Public Library, main branch, Milwaukee.
Very special thanks to Sarah Hopley, Milwaukee County Historical Society for enthusiastic support and research assistance.

Portions of this book were written by Jay W. Filter

Printed and bound in Burlington, WI

First edition

Every reasonable attempt has been made to identify owners of copyright. Errors or omissions will be corrected in subsequent editions.

ISBN 978-0-615-85707-7

Library of Congress Control Number: 2013951024

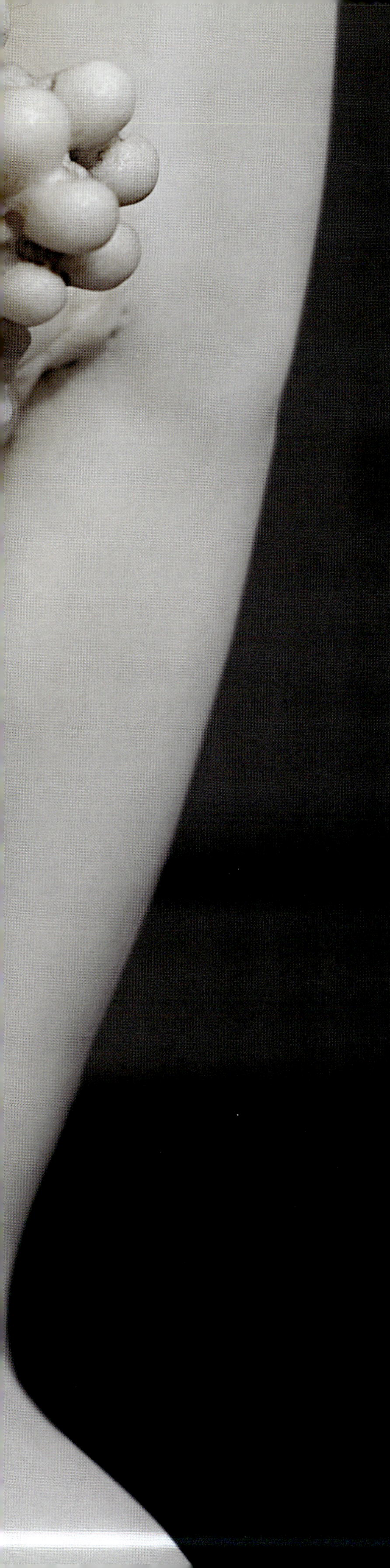

Contents

17 Introduction

25 The Pfister Hotel

53 Every Inch a Treasure

87 Fun, Relaxation and Recreation

111 Banquets & Special Happenings

135 Fine Dining, Food & Beverage

169 Quiet Comfort. Consummate Repose.

193 Taking a Closer Look

221 Every Moment a Memory

253 A History of Fine Art

269 The City, Right Outside Our Door

281 Acknowledgments

INTRODUCTION

My grandfather, Ben Marcus, was a business visionary. His story began in Ripon, Wisconsin where he scraped together all his money and bought an abandoned department store. He converted that building into a movie theatre. It proved to be a success and allowed him to expand into other areas. Eventually he would lead a collection of businesses that include lodging, movie theatres, hotel/resorts and restaurants.

In 1962 my grandfather and a small group of investors bought the Pfister. Anyone associated with the Pfister was aware of its fine tradition and heritage dating all the way back to 1893 when Charles Pfister, in fulfillment of his father's dream, built this hotel. But over the years it changed hands several times and by 1962 it was ready for a new vision, a new commitment, a new life.

Ben Marcus always had a keen eye for business talent. That's one of the reasons the Marcus Corporation has enjoyed so much success over the years. But my grandfather made one of his best business decisions ever. He brought in a young man to run this "new" venture.

His name is Steve Marcus. And he is my father.

Steve was an eager young man lured back from California to tackle the opportunity of a lifetime—renovate an historic hotel and make it the destination for anyone visiting the city of Milwaukee.

Steve will be the first to tell you that it was like being thrown in the deep end of the pool and told to swim. But when you don't have experience, you also don't have bad habits to break. Plus, fresh thinking often means trying a new or better approach that just might be worth the effort.

Applying a principle of "empowerment" Steve relied on the dedication and savvy of the many people throughout the years who he trusted to help guide the day-to-day operations.

Little by little, more people were empowered, more progress was made, and soon the Pfister was beginning to achieve the reputation we desired. A new guest tower was built and the hotel became the gathering place for any important event in the city.

When you look at the Pfister today, you see a remarkable commitment to preserving the historic beauty and character of the original hotel. Then, we add to that our plethora of modern amenities. Making each stay here at the Pfister something to remember. This has required constant reinvestment, but we view ourselves as custodians of a local institution. That is why we say, "Every Inch a Treasure. Every Moment a Memory."

Greg Marcus with his father Steven.

Above: Ben Marcus, the visionary.

Yes we all owe a debt of gratitude, first to Ben Marcus for his vision, then also to Steve Marcus for his business sense, dedication, incredible "people skills" and passion to make this hotel the jewel that it is, and to the many associates who have become like family to us as they work tirelessly to create all the special memories our guests have come to cherish.

This book is dedicated to these fine ladies and gentlemen that have gone before me.

GREG MARCUS

THE PFISTER HOTEL

Grover Cleveland was President. The Columbian World Exhibition, better known as the Chicago World's Fair, had introduced the world's largest Ferris wheel. New Zealand became the first country in the world to grant women the right to vote. And Thomas Edison created the first motion picture.

The world was rapidly changing. Yet it was still a time when men wore bowlers, women wore corsets, and bread was three cents a loaf.

The year was 1893.

This was the year that the corner of Wisconsin Avenue and Jefferson Street, in the city of Milwaukee, became a special destination. For 1893 was the year that an entirely unique hotel first opened. A hotel that was proclaimed to be "the Grand Hotel of the West."

This was the Pfister.

Guido Pfister

Charles Pfister

Earliest known postcard of the Pfister, 1899.

Opposite, from top: The original and ornate Fern Room. Along Wisconsin Avenue in the 1900's, looking west.

Following page: View from Jefferson Street, looking south.

Guido Pfister, a local entrepreneur who was born in Germany and migrated to the United States in 1845, had a vision to create a world-class hotel that would serve as a beacon of elegance and become the symbol of the marriage of old world charm with new world technology.

The city of Milwaukee had been void of a premium hotel since the fire of 1883 destroyed the venerable Newhall House. Guido Pfister was bound and determined that Milwaukee would not only replace the Newhall, but also create a new standard of charm in the making.

Unfortunately, Guido Pfister died in 1890, shortly before construction began. It was left to his son, Charles, and Guido's daughter, Louise Vogel, to complete their father's dream. Fortunately, this was a dream that they shared passionately.

A young and talented architect, Henry C. Koch, another German immigrant who moved to Milwaukee, was commissioned to design and build this magnificent structure. Henry had already completed several other significant Milwaukee landmarks and it was determined that he would be perfect for this assignment.

No expense was spared. In fact, the final cost was over a million dollars, a sum that, as of that date, far exceeded the cost of building any other hotel in the world.

But the overriding sentiment from all who experienced this new wonder was that every dollar spent was well worth it. The public and architectural critics marveled at the Richardson Romanesque style with its construction of limestone, cream-colored bricks and buff terra-cotta. People from all walks of life were captivated by the ornate lobby, with the soaring ceiling, exquisite chandeliers, and detailed ironwork of the railings and staircases. And they were stunned by the most impressive collection of original art to ever adorn a hotel: a collection that Charles Pfister had personally gathered over the years.

Fern Room, Hotel Pfister, Milwaukee.

A bustling Wisconsin Avenue with streetcars alongside horses and buggies, circa 1895.

WHO WERE THE PFISTERS?

Guido Pfister was born in Hechingen, Germany, in 1818. He learned the tanning business in his native Germany and moved to the United States in 1845, settling in Milwaukee in 1847. Incorporating his tanning skills he established a small leather store that eventually became the Guido Pfister Tanning Company. In 1872 the name was changed to the Pfister and Vogel Leather Company, soon to become one of the largest leather companies in the Midwest.

Although he was reaping the rewards of several successful entrepreneurial endeavors, Guido Pfister had more than just a passion for business. He also had a dream. That dream was to create a hotel that was so magnificent, so grand, so elegant, that it would be viewed as the premiere hotel, not just in Milwaukee, but everywhere.

Guido Pfister passed away in 1889. But his dream didn't die. For all of his aspirations and dreams were still incorporated into the plans of his magnificent hotel, as his son Charles carried forward the vision his father shared with him to create "the Gateway to the West."

Over the next few years, Charles, also a very resourceful businessman, acquired a fortune. With his fortune he was able to indulge in several prominent investments, one of which was the purchase of the *Milwaukee Sentinel* newspaper. The other? The construction of the hotel that bore his family name.

It was indeed fortunate that Charles had amassed so much money, because the construction of the Pfister Hotel was completed in 1893 at a cost of over one million dollars. When you consider that a loaf of bread cost about three cents in 1893, you can begin to appreciate just how much was invested into this magnificent hotel. And not just the construction alone. Charles had a keen eye for fine art and travelled the world to gather the finest collection of art to ever be on display in a hotel anywhere.

When Charles passed away in 1927, the Pfister Hotel had already earned the reputation as to where dignitaries, heads of state, prominent business people, and Hollywood legends preferred to rest their heads whenever a trip to Milwaukee was on their itinerary.

Clockwise from top right: The magnificent tomb of the Pfister family within Forest Home Cemetery, Milwaukee.

A beautifully engraved envelope promoting the Pfister featuring a trumpeting angel and Milwaukee's lovely coastline.

A handsome piece of hotel stationery.

Pocket-sized directory of fine hotels of the age, featuring the Pfister on its cover.

An exquisitely engraved invitation to honor European Royalty.

THE ARCHITECT
HENRY C. KOCH

Born in 1841, in Hanover, Germany, Henry C. Koch came to America and settled in Milwaukee, becoming one of the city's premiere architects. His first accomplishment of note was at age twenty-nine when he designed the Calvary Presbyterian Church, incorporating a Gothic Revival style. This was followed by the creation of Turner Hall in 1882 and the University of Wisconsin Science Hall in 1888.

In 1890, Koch began the building of the Pfister Hotel. He teamed up with a younger partner, H.J. Esser, who supervised the entire project. This Victorian masterpiece was one of their company's claims to fame and became one of their proudest accomplishments.

After completion of the Pfister, the Koch Company was commissioned to design Milwaukee's City Hall in 1895. In May of 1910, Henry Koch passed away, leaving the state of Wisconsin with some of the incredible, timeless structures that we still marvel at today.

Photograph of the newly built Pfister Hotel, looking northwest.

Warmth and elegance from the very same vantage point, over one hundred years apart.

Present day, to a day gone by. Beauty and serenity never go out of style.

Clockwise from top: Lounging in luxury in the swingin' 60's. | Owner Ben Marcus with Milwaukee's "Singing Mayor," Henry W. Maier, breaking ground for the impressive new Pfister Tower. | A pair of complementary in-room postcards showing the age of elegance, and one with the look of the future.

Opposite: The then newly-completed Pfister Tower, sitting high atop the glamorous seventh floor banquet and meeting facilities, as well as the ample parking structure.

The Pfister added some "leading edge" technology that put it way ahead of its time, such as becoming an all-electric lighted facility. At the time, gas lamps were still used and while electricity was being included, it had yet to completely replace the old gas fixtures. Charles Pfister decided that every light, every fixture, every chandelier would be powered by electricity.

And the Pfister had another notable first: individual temperature controls in every guest room. This was something virtually unheard of in the late 1800's. But, fortunately, Johnson Controls, the company pioneering this technology, was headquartered in Milwaukee. It's often been said that the Pfister Hotel was one of the primary laboratories for the new devices and inventions initiated by Johnson Controls.

Over the years the Pfister went through several changes-of-hand and many new wrinkles and enhancements.

Ray Smith, from bellhop to general manager

A young man named Ray Smith came to work for Charles Pfister in 1896. He started as a bellhop, became clerk of the cigar store, was promoted to manager of that same cigar store and eventually moved up to general manager of the hotel and heir apparent to the Pfister family. The Smith family ran the hotel until the late 1950's. After that, the Pfister struggled with new owners, including a group of New York investors who bought controlling interest and tried to manage the hotel from New York. Gradually, the Pfister started to show the signs of age and neglect. It needed a new spark. It needed a new life. It needed a new owner.

Fortunately, it wasn't just the Pfister family that had a vision for the greatness and potential of a world-class hotel in Milwaukee. The Marcus family had the same vision, the same passion and the same love and commitment to make the Pfister the "jewel" it was always destined to be.

In 1962, Ben Marcus bought controlling interest in the Pfister. One of his first, and best, decisions was to put his son Steve in charge of running this "new" Marcus venture. And Steve will be the first to tell you that his initial reaction about the prospect of leading the charge was anything but enthusiastic because he had no hotel management experience. But Ben was wise. He knew his son was smart, innovative and ready for a challenge. Ben knew that Steve would find a way. He told him, "Son...you will make mistakes. Just make sure they're not big mistakes."

By trial and error Steve Marcus gradually grew into the role of one of the most successful grand hotel owners in the world. Under his guidance the incredible artwork was restored. The new tower was completed. The marvelous ceiling lobby was reconfigured. From revamping every chandelier to modernizing every guest bathroom, Steve marshaled the resources to not just restore, but completely refurbish, the Pfister Hotel to the greatness it displays today.

Top: Something special to remember your visit: a beautifully designed, early century souvenir item.

Bottom: Charming early era, in-room thermometer. Notice, it would cost you $2.50 per night to stay—with a bath!!

Every Inch a Treasure

A nicely dressed young woman in her early twenties, sunglasses resting on top of her blond hair, approaches the front desk and picks up a newspaper. A family, father, mother and three young girls, the youngest in a stroller pushed by the father, engages the concierge in an elaborate and animated conversation, with the two older daughters doing most of the gesturing. Two elegantly dressed gentleman stand off to the side of the desk as a bellman delivers a large suitcase to each of them.

These are just a couple casual observations while strolling through the nine thousand square foot lobby of the Pfister Hotel.

If you stop and take a good look around there's always more to see; such as the people who slowly admire the marble steps of the stunning stairway, or those who casually relax in armchairs in the lobby gazing up at the mural on the ceiling or perhaps, catching the glimpse of a child rubbing the nose of one of the golden-colored lions.

And while there always seems to be plenty of people "coming and going" there are always a lot of others "stopping to notice." Because there is just so much to see and experience in one of the most elegant hotel lobbies in America.

To the first-time visitor it can be an overwhelming, yet very welcoming, feeling.

And it begins when you step out of your car or taxi and experience your initial glimpse of this magnificent structure. Looking up you'll see a massive portico with enormous granite columns and stone, topped by Romanesque ornamentations. Stepping through the entrance door, held open by a smiling attendant, and entering the lobby is like walking into another world. Everywhere you look your eyes are greeted by elegance and carefully crafted beauty.

Top: Arriving in 1970's style

Right: Always a friendly smile to greet each Pfister Hotel guest.

Opposite: Decorative ornamentation of the hotel's gorgeous and historic lobby.

Looking to your right as you enter the lobby, you may notice the comfy couches arranged around the elaborate gas fireplace. This is the original fireplace that dates all the way back to 1893. (Yes, it has always been gas…one of the questions constantly asked by visitors.) In front of the fireplace, in a checkerboard square, you can see a small section of marble floor. This is from the original marble that once graced the entire first floor of the lobby. And in the corner is an older Steinway piano. For years, this piano has been the instrument for countless afternoons and evenings of entertainment. It's been said that the late entertainer Robert Goulet and friends would spontaneously appear in late evenings and engage the guests in elaborate sing-alongs.

Also in this enclave is the old wooden bar, dating back decades, that still serves the cocktail of your choice in a most relaxing atmosphere. Two bronze statues called the "Pikemen" dating back to the opening of the hotel, stand on each side of the entrance, almost as if to greet guests on their way to the bar. These impressive "sentries" were a gift from T.A. Chapman, the famous owner of the former Chapman's stores. They originally stood beside Mr. Chapman's three-sided fireplace.

Clockwise from top right: One of the "Pikesmen" guarding the Pfister lobby.

Early century postcard of the original lobby, now used as the Pfister lounge area.

Wide-angle view of the lobby sitting and lounge area.

Fanciful and uniquely sculpted lamps adorn the lobby bar.

Opposite: Hidden in plain sight: the gorgeous relief carving inside the lobby's fireplace.

From top: One of the delightfully decorative faces found throughout the main floor.

A curious face wonders if you'll have the "time" to discover him amongst the hotel's hidden gems.

Simple, yet elegant. A wrought floret embellishes one of the Pfister's many unique furniture items.

Opposite: One of the imposing sentries stands ready for inspection.

Approaching the Victorian front desk, virtually the same intricately carved, wooden desk that has greeted guests since 1893, you begin to notice even more. You'll feel compelled to gaze up at the mural on the top of the forty-foot ceiling. Originally, the ceiling was ornate glass, which was replaced by this beautiful mural of a heavenly scene with cherubs, the creation of Conrad Schmitt Studios in Milwaukee. Look closely and you will notice that the faces of the young angels are not just the typical white faces you might see in a Michelangelo or Raphael. This was a special touch enhanced much more recently by Steve Marcus to incorporate diversity, and signal to the world that everyone is welcome at the Pfister.

In fact, at both ends of the lobby you'll find the simple word "Salve" ornately printed on the walls. The word is Latin for "hello and welcome," the very same greeting which visitors would see when the doors first opened in 1893.

Inset: Vintage key fob with embossed *Salve* crest.

Below: A lovely, heraldic hand carved face graces the lobby.

THE "FRONT"

Behind the ornate front desk that dates back to the early 1900's, you will be greeted by knowledgeable, helpful people that will be happy to accommodate all your wishes.

If you desire historical information, special assistance, directions, ticket availability or nearly anything else that would make your stay that much more rewarding or entertaining, just look to the right. There you will find the Concierge station, tucked just outside the entrance to the Café Rouge.

Gracious and inviting faces at the front desk always await each guest of the Pfister.

One of the original guest registers from the glory days of the hotel's past.

The original metal engraver's block of the hotel's exterior used for printing various hotel ephemeral items, such as letterhead, hotel bills, room stationery, etc.

When facing the front desk, if you glance to your left, you will notice the beginning of the elaborate staircase that has charmed visitors since the hotel first opened. At the base of the stairs are two golden lions, affectionately nicknamed "Dick and Harry," another gift to Charles Pfister from T. A. Chapman, who bought the lions in Italy. For thirty-three years the lions stood outside the Wisconsin Avenue side entrance to the hotel, and were relocated inside in 1926.

Moving up the stairs introduces yet another dimension to the Pfister experience.

In addition to the exquisite marble on the steps of the wide stairway you'll notice the intricate railings that grace these steps. This beautiful metal work, and the sturdy steel beams that support the stairs, are the handiwork of the original artisans of J. G. Wagner and Company of Milwaukee. Known as one of the very best for structural steel and bridge building, the company also employed special craftsmen to construct the "old German" style balustrade and newel post designs of the railings and banisters.

At the first landing you'll find two engaging paintings of two very distinctively different women. The painting on the eastern wall is simply called "Breakfast," and depicts a simple, yet elegant serving maid. The other is called "Ninon De Lenclos," and captures the image of one of the famous 17th century heartthrobs of the French court.

Clockwise from top: Early twentieth century photograph of the hotel's main lobby (looking south).

Fashionable arrivals, conversing in the lobby, shortly before the ceiling mural was commissioned.

A freshly redesigned, whiter, decor was trend of the day in the latter part of the last century.

THE TIME CAPSULE

In the middle of the main lobby you'll find a small square pillar with a plaque. Sealed inside are a wide variety of artifacts dating back as far as 1894.

The purpose of the capsule is to share with the future the rich history of the Pfister past, not to be opened until 2093, the two hundred year anniversary of the hotel.

Packed inside are over one hundred and fifty different items, including a print advertisement for the hotel from 1894, a copy of a letter from Charles Pfister to the hotel's switchboard operator in 1908, a ticket to the Charles Lindberg Day reception in 1927, menus from every era and personal letters from Ben and Steve Marcus.

It is the hope of everyone at the Pfister that the hotel will be every bit as vital in 2093, ready for another time capsule to take its place.

Dick and Harry, the Pfister lions, stand watch over the lobby.

One of the "servidors" as seen throughout the original side of the Pfister.

The acclaimed father of the Pfister's rebirth, redesign and revitalization, Ben Marcus.

Moving up to the second landing reveals a double tribute to the late Ben Marcus, the man who purchased the Pfister in 1962 and began the massive restoration. You'll find both a very lifelike bronze bust and an oil portrait reminding people who walk these steps of the person who made it all possible today.

The second floor of the Pfister offers a welcome surprise. On the east side you'll notice how wide the hallway is and what a glorious view it affords of the lobby below. This was the promenade, a place for brides, dignitaries, and the fashionable, to be "seen." Along the outside walls you'll notice the hotel room doors equipped with an original Milwaukee invention, the "servidor." This was a part of the modernization during the 1929 renovation and was intended to allow the ladies and gentlemen a safe, secure and private way to have their clothes that need cleaning placed in the door and retrieved by a staff member without ever having to open the room door.

And on the walls you'll see more and more of the original paintings that Charles Pfister purchased in the late 1800's. In fact, one of the charms of the Pfister is walking the hallways and taking in the eighty-plus works of art that grace each hallway, each banquet room and every nook and cranny.

THE LOBBY PIANO

If you walk by the lobby early in the day you might not even notice the piano in the corner near the window. It's not the size of a grand piano, but it's a little bit bigger than a baby grand. It's black. And it's old. In fact, this piano dates back to nearly the opening of the hotel.

It's called an Apollo. If you happen to be a music buff, that alone will make your ears perk up, for the Apollo pianos were hand crafted in New York in the late 1800's. Today, they are a rare find.

But even if you're not a music aficionado, the moment a pair of talented hands touch the keys you will be amazed. Especially if the hands belong to Dr. Jeffrey Hollander. Dr. Hollander has been the resident pianist at the Pfister since the early 1980's. And magic happens when he makes music. One of the most gifted musicians this city has ever seen, Dr. Hollander has been entertaining audiences since he was a child.
In fact, he won a scholarship to the Eastman School of Music. He was seven years old.

Dr. Hollander and the Apollo are perfectly matched for each other. He knew it the first time he sat at the bench and touched the keys. "What a live, beautiful sound!" he exclaimed.

Dr. Jeffrey Hollander

Fun, Relaxation & Recreation
Then & Now

In the late 1800's, few people could afford the opportunity to pamper themselves. Life was tougher, in general, and personal self-indulgence was often frowned upon.

But when people travel, then, and now, they like to take the opportunity to surround themselves with amenities they usually don't encounter in everyday life.

Back in the early 1900's, the Pfister was the place where people could enjoy some of the luxuries of fun, comfort and sport they might not find anywhere else.

One of the hotel's two sophisticated billiard rooms.

Opposite: A few pieces of Pfister memorabilia from the hotel's former cigar stand and lounge on the first floor.

The early Pfister actually had two billiard rooms. One for the men and one for the women. Billiards actually began about the 15th century and started as a lawn game somewhat similar to croquet. When they moved the game inside, a green cloth was incorporated to simulate the grass. The original tables had flat walls for rails and helped keep the balls on the table. It was said they resembled riverbanks. Once people discovered that they could use the walls to bounce balls in a desired direction, the term "bank shot" came into being.

This popular game was a big hit at the Pfister. In fact, the Brunswick company designed a one-of-a-kind billiards table for the hotel that became the prototype for one of their best-selling models.

There were two billiards rooms. One for the men and one for the women.

And, especially for the men, nothing added to a feeling of total relaxation like enjoying a good cigar. Fortunately, the Pfister had one of the Midwest's best, most elaborate, and original cigar stores. Covering nearly the entire area that is today the main reception desk in the lobby, travelers, and people from all over the city, found this the best destination for "a good smoke." In fact, one of the most popular brands was the "Pfister Special," a unique blend all their own. The cigar store was also the stepping-stone for Ray Smith, eventual successor of Charles Pfister, as owner of the hotel. Ray successfully ran the store for years and that led to further promotions in management that eventually resulted in landing him at the top.

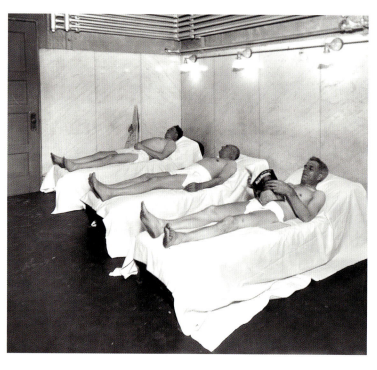

Above: A trio of pictures showing both proud Pfister employees, and their relaxed, contented customers taking advantage of the hotel's world-class features.

Below: A charming barbershop amenity, likely a vessel to hold combs or scissors.

A short walk downstairs from the lobby afforded the gentlemen another luxury that the Pfister provided: one of the most successful barbershops in the city. With twelve chairs ready and waiting, you didn't have to wait long for your hot towel, fresh shave and professional haircut.

And it was affordable.

There was a time when a shave and a haircut actually cost just two bits.

The ladies were invited as well for shampoos, haircuts and manicures. For the men, right across the way, they could enjoy the Turkish bath.

Today, the barbershop is gone. The billiard tables are in storage. And the cigar store is a memory. But now that short walk downstairs from the lobby reveals a whole new world of relaxation, pampering and grooming.

Welcome to the world of the Pfister Well Spa and Salon.

It's not unusual to experience encounters with well-known people in the spa of the Pfister. Like hearing a famous sixties rocker softly singing as the manicurist put rainbows on her nails. Or hearing one of our country's iconic crooners humming along to his iPod as he runs on the treadmill in the exercise room. You might run into any number of NBA stars in long robes emerging from a deep massage for a strained back. Or even well-known major league baseball pitchers having a manicure to fix their damaged cuticles that might impede the proper spin of their curve ball.

S A L O N

From top: Stunning and ornate mirror adoring the Well Spa's reception area

All the colors of the rainbow from which to choose.

Opposite: The salon awaits your first class experience.

Yes, many, many famous people have enjoyed the exquisite personal touches and expertise of the Pfister Well Spa and Salon. But true to the Pfister philosophy, all people are treated as celebrities. Unlike other spas where you might have to share a locker room, here you get your own private suite.

The Spa boasts thirty-five talented associates that can provide anything from a mud bath to hammam showers, haircuts, perms, trims, pedicures... just about any pampering you can imagine. There are even group rooms for bridal parties and doubles for couples looking for something special. In fact, several people have used this as an opportunity to propose marriage. Something the staff is happy to accommodate.

103

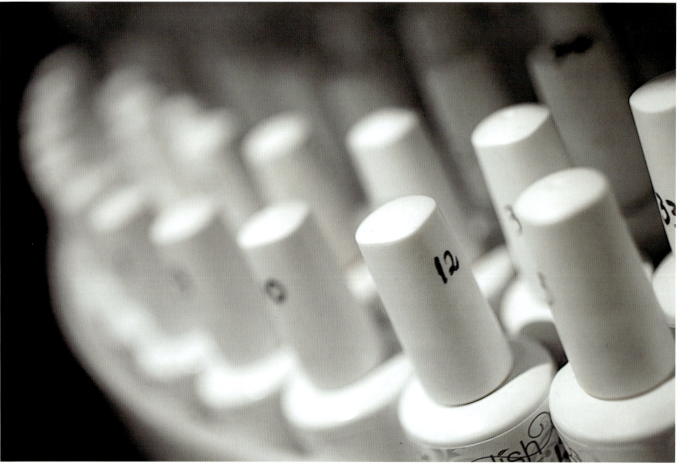

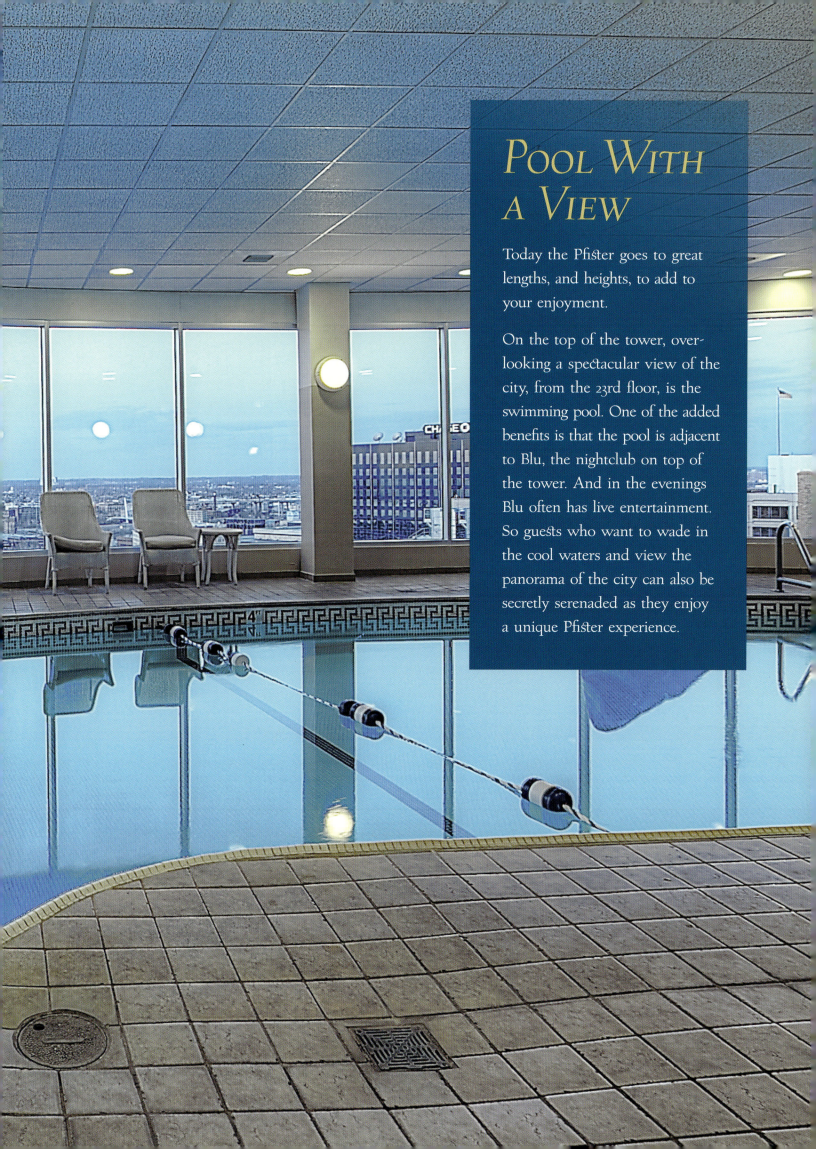

Pool With a View

Today the Pfister goes to great lengths, and heights, to add to your enjoyment.

On the top of the tower, overlooking a spectacular view of the city, from the 23rd floor, is the swimming pool. One of the added benefits is that the pool is adjacent to Blu, the nightclub on top of the tower. And in the evenings Blu often has live entertainment. So guests who want to wade in the cool waters and view the panorama of the city can also be secretly serenaded as they enjoy a unique Pfister experience.

Banquets & Special Happenings

"Beware of Bride." This seems to be the attitude of so many places that cater to large parties and weddings.

The Pfister is the opposite.

"This is the biggest moment of a bride's life, of course she's going to need extra hand holding and understanding…that's what we're here for." This explanation was from Rosie DeRubertis, retired head of catering and forty year employee of the Pfister.

"We do everything we can to make this moment as stress free and wonderful as she, and her family, expects."

Above: Cover of early 1900's souvenir book compliments of Charles Pfister.

Right: Banquet room set up for wedding with arch, flowers and ceremonial cups.

There have been challenges. Like the time the bride insisted her friend, who had taken a class on cake making, supply the wedding cake. When she tried to assemble the cake she forgot the supporting pillars and everything collapsed into a mess on the floor.

"I told the chef to pull every dessert he could find out of the freezer and we served that. Everyone enjoyed the meal. You just can't panic in situations like that." DeRubertis said.

Sometimes the only solution is to appeal to reason.

"One bride showed up a week before her event and insisted that the carpeting in the ballroom would clash with the bridesmaids' dresses and wanted us to replace it. We explained how the room would be filled with tables and linen and flowers and that no one would notice the floor. It took quite some persuading but eventually she changed her mind and had a beautiful wedding."

And sometimes you have to just get creative.

"One year we had so many weddings that some people had to settle for the smallest ballroom, which usually seats about a hundred and twenty five," DeRubertis recalls. " We had three hundred and twenty five people show up in that little room for dinner...and dancing. It was tight and we had to be on our toes but we served dinner, then removed the tables, put down the dance floor, and everyone had a delightful time."

And you can't overlook the avid sports fans.

"Years back, before everyone had phones that could give you sports scores, before televisions could be easily accessed, one group wanted a television in the ballroom to watch Marquette basketball. At the time there was no cable connection in the ballrooms. Maintenance found a way to rig something up and, sure enough, a lot of the wedding party was watching basketball."

This "can do" attitude is one of the reasons the Pfister hosts over a hundred weddings a year and countless corporate events.

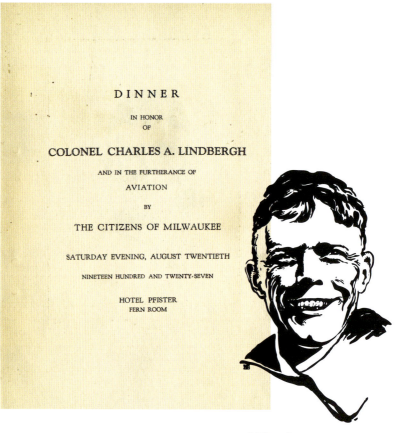

"The American Boy"

Each of the banquet rooms seems alive with history. It's as if you can almost see the great actress Lillian Russell holding court as she entertains her entire theatre company with a special holiday party. Or perhaps you can feel the far away presence of Sarah Bernhard or the more recent vibrations of the Bob Hope or Vince Lombardi Galas held in the not too distant past.

And the Pfister can always brag about being the hotel that had the rare opportunity to honor three of America's greatest aviators: Charles Lindbergh, Wiley Post, and Douglas "Wrong Way" Corrigan.

From political gathering to corporate events and weddings, the Pfister has the reputation for really being able to pull out all the stops.

In fact, some of the most famous people in the world have graced the banquet rooms of the Pfister.

Because the Pfister has had a reputation for *quality, comfort and elegance*, it has attracted more than a fair share of celebrities.

There have been hundreds and hundreds of celebrities that have stayed at the Pfister over the years. That includes nearly every United States President since McKinley, every major rock star, world dignitaries, and dozens of well-known actresses and actors.

But you seldom hear about them.

There's a reason for that.

It is Pfister policy that no hotel employee can make any mention of a celebrity in attendance until that celebrity had been gone for at least a day. And then, and only then, can they casually mention that a movie, sports or rock star, high-ranking government official or Saudi prince happened to be here. There are no photographs, autographs or intrusive interventions allowed.

Why so strict?

This is one of the reasons that well-known people enjoy staying at the Pfister; they are treated as royally as all the guests and yet can feel practically anonymous while here.

Even today, the feeling is, if a celebrity grants express permission, they might share a story or two, but otherwise, unless it happened in the distant past, they won't mention to anyone about the incredible "who's who" that have graced this hotel.

So, who did stay here back in the day? What stories can be shared?

How about Elvis?

"It was almost as if he were president of the United States," says Rosemary Steinfest, the retired General Manager of the Pfister.

"His entourage would be on the phone announcing that he was fifteen minutes away…then ten…then five…then there he was getting out of the limo

Above: A magnificent invitation and a colorful program welcoming world-famous Guests of Honor.

Opposite, from top: One of the hotel's spectacular ballrooms and its packed-house of distinguished gentlemen ready for the wow-factor.

Souvenir program honoring an American hero, Charles A. Lindbergh.

on the seventh floor of the parking ramp with a crowd attending. He had a drink in his hand so I opened the door for him. He was so appreciative and nice and polite."

He did insist his favorite bacon be flown in and cooked whenever he wanted.

Neil Diamond was a big fan of ping-pong. "We converted the second floor conference room. We put down a wood floor, raised the chandeliers and put in the table. It was what he wanted," Steinfest added.

Luciano Pavoratti was a stickler for pasta. He insisted on freshly made pasta and, fortunately, Rosemary DeRubertis, retired head of catering, had a friend that had opened a business making fresh pasta. "It obviously met with his approval. He gave me ten tickets to the performance that was to be held that evening. In the front row! I wasn't sure I could get ten people on such short notice. But everyone I called said 'yes' and we felt like he was singing just to us."

Carol Channing, the renowned star of Broadway and films, insisted her room be decorated like the set of "Hello Dolly."

Every President of the United States since McKinley has stayed here (Barack Obama was here...but as a U.S. Senator). It was here at the Pfister that former president Taft was staying when he woke in the morning to the news that World War I had come to an end. Once Harry Truman, on opening the door to the Presidential Suite, looked in the room, smiled and said, "There's my old chair." And before John F. Kennedy was president, the Pfister served as his strategy headquarters while planning his election.

When Paul McCartney was in town for a concert he stayed at the Pfister and was sitting in the lobby as Dr. Jeffrey Hollander was playing the piano. "I started playing Beatles melodies and he enjoyed it very much. We had a delightful conversation," said Dr. Hollander.

Executive Chef Brian Frakes has met nearly every famous person, if for no other reason than the location of the kitchen. "You remember that scene in the movie 'Good Fellas' where the camera goes through the kitchen following Henry (Ray Liotta) and his date on the way to the nightclub? It's kind of like that. A lot of the people want a discreet way in and they cut through the kitchen. I've met quite a few stars and dignitaries that way."

So if you stay at the Pfister and wonder if that happens to be an MVP baseball player, Opera Diva or Rock Star sitting next to you at the Mason Street Grill... it just might be.

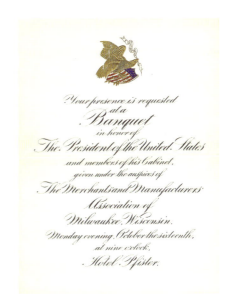

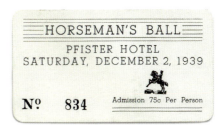

From top: "Ladies and Gentlemen, the President of the United States." No doubt the most sought after invite of that year!

Souvenir ticket from one of the many themed events over the years.

Beautifully designed hotel tableware from yesteryear.

Opposite, from top: Proud and accomplished members of the Pfister's very own "top chef" staff shown in two distinct decades of the last century.

A vintage, charming dining table accessory.

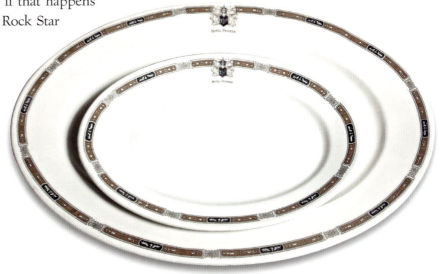

Fine Dining, Food & Beverage

The Executive Chef of the Pfister has a rather special office: It's in the basement. And it just happens to be the exact same office of the original chef in 1893. And though the cuisine may have changed dramatically over the years, one thing doesn't change: the impeccable coordination of meals to serve large groups of people.

"This is like a Swiss watch," says Executive Chef Brian Frakes. "Everyone has to be in the right place at the right time and performing their job with precision and expertise."

This helps explain how you can serve over four hundred people at one sit down meal.

Vintage postcards highlighting the different glorious dining settings

As guests enjoy their soup or appetizer, they seldom realize that nearly thirty people are behind the kitchen door preparing the entrees and desserts for every event.

"We've had a lot of practice, " Chef Frakes says with a smile.

And, based on the letters on file, a lot of compliments. And don't overlook the challenge of room service in a hotel that typically has hundreds of guests on a given night.

Fortunately for visitors, the Pfister boasts one of the most extensive room service menus offered twenty four hours a day. From full breakfasts, lunches and dinner entrées to late night specials that even include Zaffiro's pizza, one of the most famous names for pizza in Milwaukee since 1954.

Guests are seldom disappointed with the quality and speed of even some of the most unusual requests.

"We do everything we can to accommodate our guests," Frakes says, "Once we had a request for a fresh peanut butter and jelly sandwich. I mean really fresh. So we crushed up the peanuts added a little oil, whipped it up. Couldn't be much fresher. And the guest was simply delighted."

But in addition to serving incredible meals for banquets and weddings, the Pfister has always provided guests and local residents the opportunity to experience fine dining in a restaurant adjacent to the hotel. For many years that was a short walk downstairs to the English Room.

Back in the sixties and seventies, people were treated to exquisite meals with much of it prepared right at their tableside. Many a birthday or anniversary was celebrated here.

Blanke's Coffee used the Pfister in one of its ads, stating the hotel was "One of the very best in the United States."

The English Room: the Pfister's world-famous restaurant, now just a memory, featured the skilled Maitre d' hotel, Frank Bonfiglio.

Opposite: The brilliant, new, and in-demand Mason Street Grill, brainchild of Greg Marcus.

Mason Street Grill, at the ready.

Opposite: The Mason Street Grill's counter seating, providing guests with an up-close dining experience, not soon forgotten

Today, the Mason Street Grill has replaced the English Room as the Pfister's premiere restaurant. Located on the first floor with street access on Mason and Jefferson streets, the Mason Street Grill has consistently ranked as one of the most preferred restaurants in the city. But then, Mason Street provides some exceptional "extras" that you won't find in other restaurants. Like their unique gas/charcoal/wood burning stove. This stove provides the flexibility necessary to deliver the unique flavors only a live fire can provide. It was specially made in Washington, D.C., just for this restaurant.

In addition, by special request, some lucky diners have been invited to visit the wine cellar in the basement. Here, in a temperature-controlled vault, you'll find a selection that varies from everyday to extraordinary. This offering is so impressive that the *Wine Spectator* magazine has consistently bestowed the Mason Street Grill with the "*Wine Spectator* Award of Excellence."

The bar of the Mason Street Grill has become an evening magnet for anyone interested in live music, from contemporary to jazz. Many nights you'll discover a wide range of superb entertainers, including the likes of Wynton Marsalis or Al Jarreau.

If you want to enjoy the Pfister at its finest, Sunday Brunch in the Rouge banquet room is certainly on the list of "must do's." This elegant, open, first floor room with high ceiling and natural woodwork is the perfect setting for that special occasion meal with chef-prepared entries, fresh salads, carving and action stations and decadent desserts. And, if so inclined, enjoy a champagne toast or a spicy Bloody Mary.

This brunch is so popular, there are some that come here on a weekly basis.

And for the casual, quick or simply convenient breakfast or lunch, you can't beat the Café at the Pfister. The moment you walk through the door you'll see some of the most tempting pastries and scones, made fresh by the Pfister baking staff. Add to that fresh-brewed coffee, featuring Starbucks original, provided by the eager barista. Of course, full breakfast and lunch meals are available in the comfortable dining room.

If in the mood to just relax and unwind, the Pfister has that covered as well, starting with the main lobby bar. Sit back in one of the cushy, comfortable chairs and be served the cocktail of your choice. This is one of the best "people watching" areas in the hotel, as you have a view of the many different people from all walks of life on their way to, or from, a game, concert, play or night on the town. And if you're fortunate enough to be there after 5 p.m., you'll be entertained by a live piano performance. For nearly three decades that entertainment has been provided by the one-and-only Dr. Jeffrey Hollander. Dr. Hollander has been hailed as one of the most talented pianists in the entire Midwest. From Bach to the Beatles, he swiftly blends one melody into another. Truly enjoyable.

Unwind Up Top

To move up-tempo, simply move upstairs, to the 23rd floor of the tower. That is where you'll find Blu, the nightclub that offers some of the most magnificent vistas of the city and lake. Sip a glass of wine, a draft beer or expertly mixed cocktail and enjoy the lively sounds of some of the area's best live entertainment.

And Blu also offers something you just won't find in any other hotel in the area, Afternoon Tea. During the winter months guests can enjoy the warmth of the fireplace and a tableside tea blending, presented in all-silver service by a Pfister Tea Butler. Of course, fresh scones, sandwiches and pastries are offered as well.

All in all, the Pfister offers a unique combination of dining and entertaining experiences. And this is one of the reasons so many guests return again...and again.

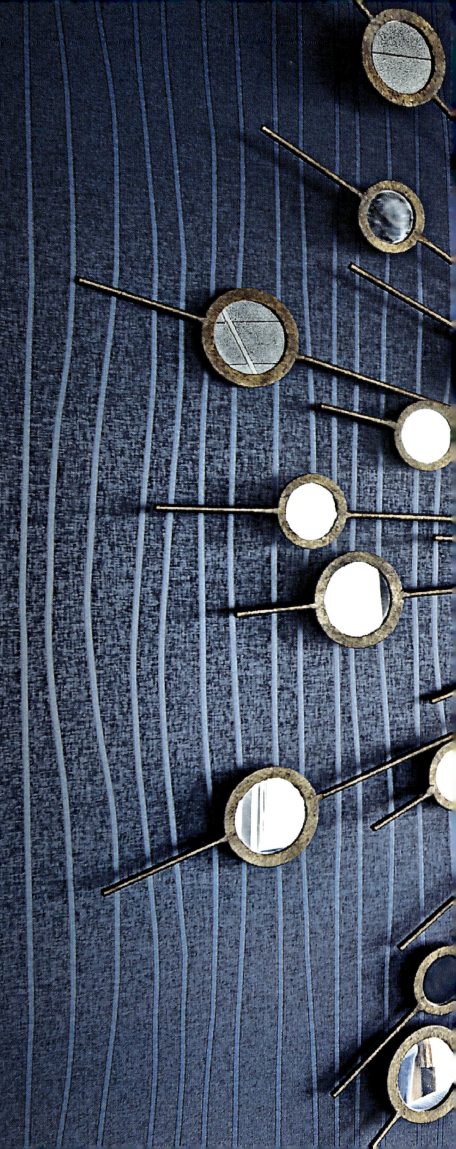

Quiet Comfort.
Consummate Repose.

When all is said and done, the most important part of any hotel stay is how much you enjoyed your room. Was it comfortable? Was it quiet? Was it clean? Did you feel like you belonged? Were you well served?

At the Pfister, throughout history, the entire staff has strived to make the answer to each of those questions a resounding "Yes!"

Over the years, some of the letters received have been affirmation that they've done a pretty good job of making people feel like this truly is "the palace for the people."

One of the challenges of the Pfister has been to make sure they maintain their "old world charm" without overlooking the modern amenities that travelers demand today.

Early photograph of one of the Pfister's splendid and comfortable rooms.

Some of the services provided in the past were essential, at the time, but outdated today. For instance, some of the guests choose to forgo the valet services that will pick up and clean or press their clothes with incredibly quick turnaround. Like so many people today they even choose to iron their own clothes. And for them, an iron and board can be found in the closet. A hundred years ago, an iron had to be heated on a stove and brought to the room. One story has it that one particular guest who couldn't sleep wanted to iron, all night. The staff, always attentive, brought this guest at least seven irons in one evening.

As a matter of course, room service has always been one of the hallmarks of the Pfister. And that service means a lot more than just delivering food to the door. Because it is their mission to always find a way to accommodate even some of the most challenging requests.

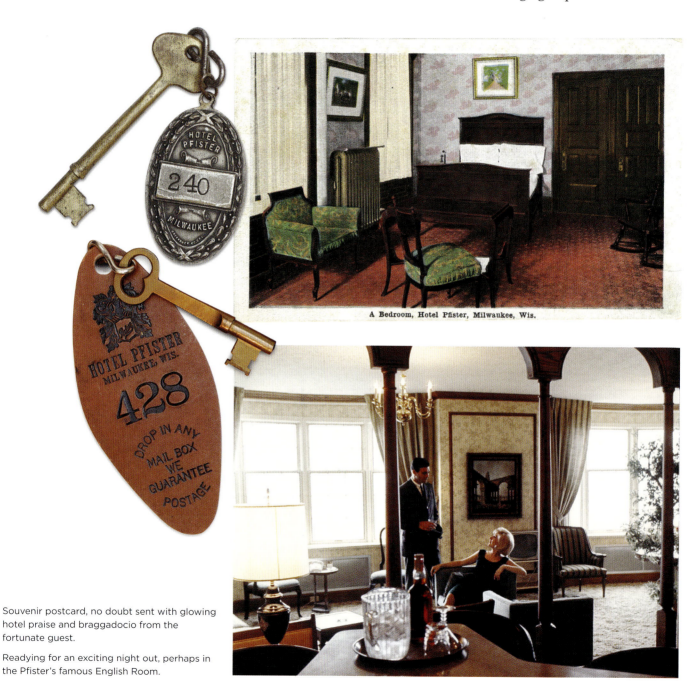

A Bedroom, Hotel Pfister, Milwaukee, Wis.

Souvenir postcard, no doubt sent with glowing hotel praise and braggadocio from the fortunate guest.

Readying for an exciting night out, perhaps in the Pfister's famous English Room.

For instance, one guest would ship his own personal showerhead to the hotel before his arrival. The staff would install it and it would be ready to go when the guest showed up. Afterwards, the staff would dismantle the showerhead and ship it back to him.

Some guests insist on total darkness. For them, foil is put on the windows and a cut out of wood placed over each window frame.

A few people can bring new meaning to the concept of service, like traveling with their own chef. (Luciano Pavoratti certainly did.) If and when that happens, accommodations are made so that their chefs have a place in the kitchen just for them.

In days of old and in keeping with many European hotel traditions of the time, the Pfister had individual hotel rooms that shared common bathrooms. It wasn't unusual to see a hotel guest in his robe and slippers knocking on a door to see if it was his turn for a bath. Today, not only does every room offer a private bathroom, the modern fixtures and accommodations look like they belong in an architectural magazine.

Which brings up an interesting debate: Do you prefer the tower or the historic section of the building?

There are pluses to both. On the historic side you get wider hallways graced with exquisite artwork, taller windows in the room and easier access to the lobby. In the tower, your room is more modern, you have more window light, and on the higher floors, you have a commanding view of the city.

Both sides benefit from an impeccably picky service staff that insists the linen and towels are fresh and clean and the toiletries are of spa quality. And all the linens, bedding, and towels are of the highest quality. In addition, from make-up mirrors to full-length mirrors, iPod docks, and coffee makers, to room safes and flat screen TVs, the Pfister doesn't just meet your expectations for a luxury hotel, it often exceeds them.

Guestroom amenities, old and new.

THE *PFISTER* EXPERIENCE HAS PROVEN TO BE OF SUCH EXQUISITE STYLE, COMFORT, AND LUXURY THAT THEY HAVE REPEAT CUSTOMERS FROM ALL OVER THE WORLD.

Also, for added room and comfort or very special occasions, the Pfister has mini-suites, full suites, and even three Presidential Suites. What was the original Presidential Suite on the third floor in the main building started as the Rococo Suite and became known as the Presidential Suite after President McKinley first stayed there. Many other Presidents followed. But years ago when Wisconsin's governors started using that room as their "home away from Madison," the name quickly changed to the Governor's Suite, as it is known today. In the corridor right outside this room are portraits of each Wisconsin governor.

A Bedroom, Hotel Pfister, Milwaukee, Wis.

Taking a Closer Look

When you visit Wisconsin you know that sooner or later, during the cold winter months, it's going to snow. Looking out a window, the snowfall often appears as a beautiful cascade of white that adds beauty to grey sidewalks and street lamps.

But when you take a closer look, you notice even more: You begin to see that no two snowflakes are alike. This observation also holds true for the Pfister: Look closer and you realize that no two views are alike. Scrutinize every inch of this hotel and your eyes will reveal artistry, craftsmanship and beauty everywhere you turn.

Once you enter the door of the Pfister and move inside, if you look closely, so many of the carefully planned, intimate details begin to reveal themselves. It's almost as if, according to Peter Mortensen, longtime concierge, "Wherever your eyes travel within this hotel you will be greeted by a visual treat."

Suddenly, the wrought iron on a staircase, the twisted metal on the bottom of a chair, the visual hiding behind the flames of the fireplace or the fabric pattern on a hallway sofa show themselves to you. Within every room, every lobby, every ballroom, every corner of this hotel you'll find these small, precious works of art that aren't framed and hanging on the walls.

Every Moment a Memory

No matter what your age, if you spend any amount of time with someone who is older, you'll invariably hear about the "good old days": a nonspecific era when everything seemed to be, well, just better. The quality of goods was higher, people were more cheerful and courteous, service was sharper, and conscientiousness thrived. It's become nostalgia to those people who witnessed it all, now just a sorely missed caliber of excellence forgotten in favor of progress.

Look around the Pfister. Notice anything? That's right, those very same remarkable qualities, lamented by many as gone forever, simply abound at this historic establishment; the attention to detail, service, and comfort. The staff members exude noticeable pride in a job-well-done spirit. The pleasantries are enhanced by a facility-wide positive, can-do attitude. Plus that minute-by-minute dedication to that most particular level of excellence that only world-class hospitality can boast.

It's easy to see just exactly what surrounding oneself with attentive workers, who love their jobs, can mean to a guest or visitor. Whether it's someone's first stay or fiftieth, the Pfister treats everyone as if *this* time will be that special time they'll remember forever.

Yes, the "good old days" are back again. Alive and well and waiting for all to enjoy at the world-famous Pfister Hotel.

Pfister Hotel softball team, 1939 hotel league champions.

Throughout the years the dedicated staff are rewarded by Pfister Hotel management. The 1956 Pfister employees Ten Year Club was treated to a picnic and Milwaukee Braves game.

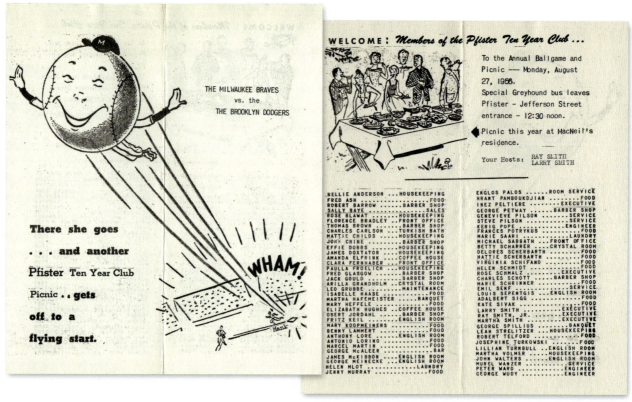

When you speak with some of its staff members, the words they most often share with you, to describe their feelings about being employed by Wisconsin's most venerable hotel, are nearly always the same: being a part of the "Pfister family."

Such personal and professional dedication has been rewarded over the years in a variety of ways, including annual staff outings, holiday parties and special events. Recently, a very special tribute was established to honor the hotel's long-tenured employees of twenty-five years or more with a celebration that includes a weekend of dining, entertainment and parties. As an extra special gift, each valued member of this momentous group receives a lifetime pass at all Marcus Movie Theaters around the Midwest!!

GIVING EVERY GUEST THE STAR TREATMENT

The term "concierge" is of French origin and roughly translates to "The Keeper of the Candles." The main duty of the Concierge was to tend to the visiting nobles in medieval castles.

According to Peter Mortensen, whose tenure as Chief Concierge began in 1986, the role of the concierge at the Pfister is to "make wishes happen." Mortensen delights in his job and has lost little of the enthusiasm that makes coming to work not a chore... but a privilege.

"You're walking the same staircase that Sarah Bernhardt walked and looking at the same paintings that Ethel Barrymore looked at!" Mortensen exclaims with great pride. "I never get tired of it because it's always alive...it's always electric!"

One of the reason Mortensen feels so many people enjoy their stay at the Pfister is the feeling that there is no "rank or title" that one guest enjoys more than another.

"We treat each and every guest as a celebrity...because in our eyes, they truly are."

Talking with some of the long-time employees invariably leads to some wonderful memories and stories of people, events and happenstance.

Chris Kanzelberger, the night manager can recall so many memorable people he's met over the years, including five world leaders.

"In the course of my duties I had the honor of meeting both presidents Bush, Jimmy Carter and even former Soviet Union president Mikhail Gorbachev and former British Prime Minister Margaret Thatcher. Each of them were very impressive," says Kanzelberger.

From rock stars, to movies stars to the rich and famous, Chris has had the privilege of meeting some of the world's most entertaining and sought-after celebrities.

"One evening," Chris offers, "we had to deliver something to one of the rooms and the maid kept telling me it was someone named 'Carum Jabber'. I had no idea that when I knocked on the door who this 'Carem Jabber' might be. Well, when a smiling seven foot three inch man answered the door I discovered that Carem Jabber was actually Kareem Abdul Jabbar."

Chris began his career at the Pfister as a lifeguard for the pool on the 23rd floor. "I remember seeing a gentleman at one end of the pool performing some water exercises. I went over and started talking and realized he had a strong foreign accent and was quite fascinating. We chatted at length. He said he was in town to perform and asked if I would like tickets to his show. Of course I gratefully accepted. As he climbed the stairs to get out of the pool he reached for two crutches. It was then that I put two and two together and realized I was going to experience the incredible talent of Itzhak Perlman."

Rocman "Roc" Whitesell, one of the Pfister concierges recalls the time the front door opened and in waltzed (literally) Sarah Ferguson, Dutchess of York. "Dr. Hollander was playing a waltz on the piano and, having been a frequent guest at the Pfister, Miss Ferguson knew us rather well," says Roc. "So when she opened her arms and beckoned me to dance with her I was flattered but had to tell her, 'I am so sorry but I am on duty.' Well, she just smiled and said, 'When a Duchess asks you to dance, you dance.' So I waltzed her over to the elevator and, to my surprise, turned back to quite a bit of applause. I was just glad I didn't trip or fall."

Roc also likes to recall the time a long limousine pulled up the hotel entrance and an older, elegantly dressed woman emerged and walked briskly to his station. "She had a cane and rapped it on the desk in front of me and gestured to the locked doors of the Café Rouge, the elegant room on our first floor. 'Young man, she said, 'open those doors.' I told her that I was sorry but that room was closed. This didn't deter her. 'Young man, I was married in that room seventy six years ago…open the doors.'"

"Well," Roc continues, "of course I let her in and she stood at the opening for the longest time and I could hear that she was singing, 'Here Comes the Bride.' After she left I asked countless people who she was and there was great speculation, but I never knew for sure."

■ ■ ■

There isn't a Pfister employee who doesn't have a story or two.
And that just makes their job that much more interesting and a big part of the reason
so many enjoy working at the Pfister for years and years.

A History of Fine Art

For many years Milwaukee has enjoyed a reputation as being a destination for those who love and appreciate fine and rare works of art. In fact, an article in the *Chicago Tribune* once reported that, "There are probably more creditable works of fine art in the collections of this city and the colony of artists is larger in proportion to the population than any other city of the United States."

Fortunately for this city, Charles Pfister was responsible for a lot of the recognition Milwaukee started to gain long ago.

Much of this is thanks to another German-born Milwaukeean, Henry Reinhardt, who was to become one of the country's most prestigious art dealers, opening galleries in Chicago, New York and Paris. Reinhardt provided a tremendous resource for Charles to fill the Pfister Hotel with much of the collection that graces the hotel to this very day.

Nearly all of the work embraces a style that was very much in vogue in the early 1900's but seems so natural and appropriate today hanging on the walls of a hotel conceived during a bygone era. The landscapes, portraits and sculptures are distributed throughout the hotel and serve as a welcome invitation at the top of each stairway or down a long corridor.

Today, the Pfister still boasts the largest collection of Victorian art of any hotel in the world. And the commitment of the Pfister to remaining a destination for art lovers continues with the "Artist in Residence" program that was launched in 2009.

This program is part of the international Alliance of Artists Communities, the service organization dedicated to the field of artists' communities, residency programs, individuals and institutions that support living artists in the creation of new work. This program covers the entire United States and more than a dozen countries worldwide.

The Pfister has renovated the former Business Center on the ground floor to serve as an open working space for each artist selected, as well as a place to display the art for enjoyment and purchase. Often, the artist can be seen working live on his or her personal genre of art right before your eyes.

Over the years the artists have varied in media from sculpture and fine art all the way to designing dresses from old cassette tapes. So, just when you think you may have seen it all, a visit to the Artist in Residence will open your eyes to something new and exciting.

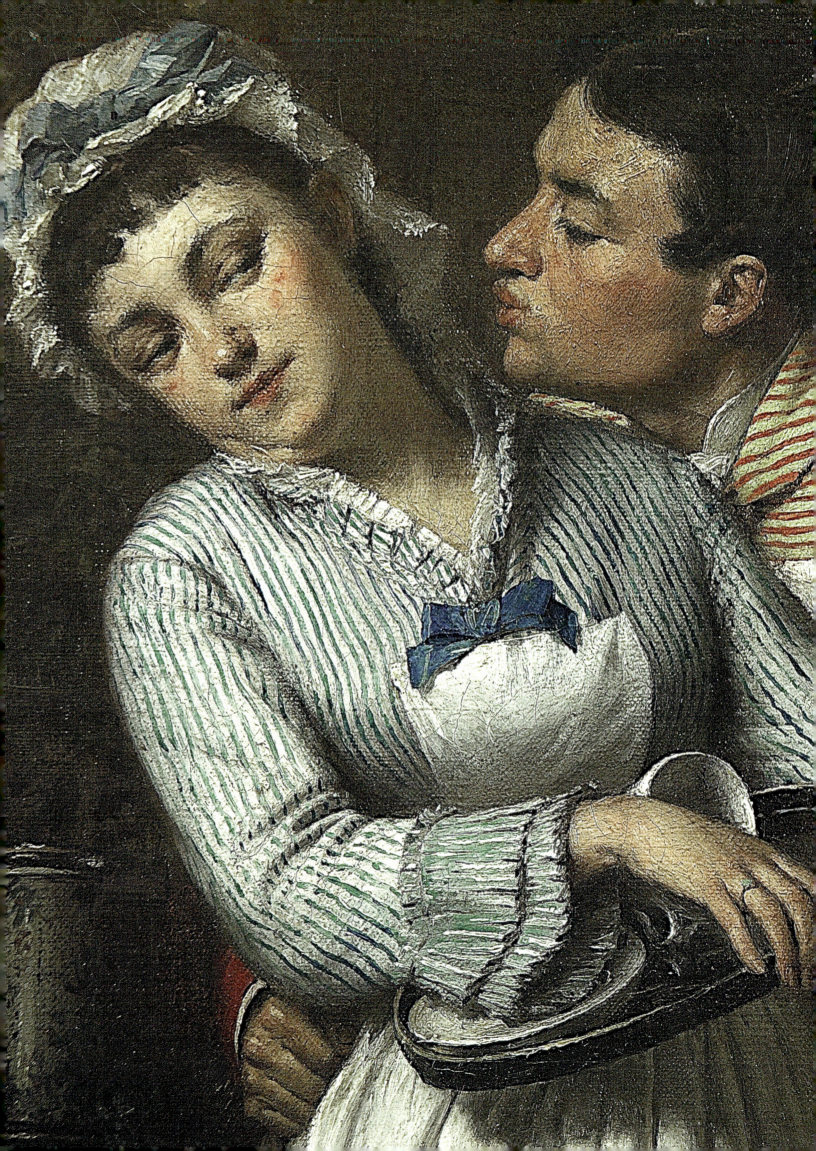

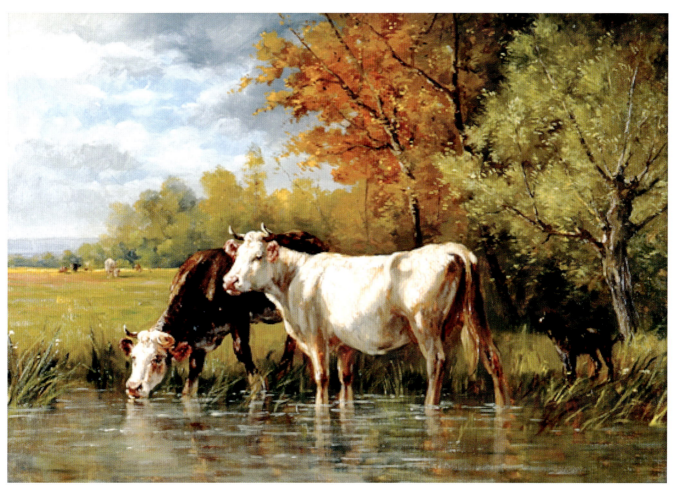

The City, Just Outside Our Door

Man does not live by bed alone. Neither does woman. Fortunately for every man, woman and child who stays at the Pfister, a myriad of impressive things to see, places to go, and stuff to do and enjoy are mere moments away.

Just east of the hotel, a few blocks down Wisconsin Avenue stands the curious and spectacular structure affectionately known as "The Calatrava." Its gigantic spanning wings rise and lower, weather permitting, on a daily basis and is officially called the "brise soleil" (french for "sun-breaker"). This marvel of modern design is the brainchild of world-famous Spanish architect, Santiago Calatrava. It's the most recent addition to the Milwaukee Art Museum and it houses the Quadracci Pavilion, as well as a restaurant, and artifacts shop. The Milwaukee Art Museum, aka MAM, contains thousands and thousands of priceless paintings, sculptures, and Objets d'Art.

The Pfister concierge will gladly assist you in putting together a truly memorable visit to some of the icons of Milwaukee.

Milwaukee Art Museum

Harley Davidson Museum

Also, not too far away, sits one of Milwaukee's, and for that matter—the country's, favorite places. The Harley Davidson Museum. Replete with the entire iconic brand's history, plus tours, exhibits, programs, events, archives, nearly five hundred hogs and artifacts, and a fabulous restaurant.

Miller Valley

Another spot closely associated with Milwaukee's rich history is the Miller-Coors Brewing Company. Just west of downtown, Miller Valley hosts the original brewing facilities, including the actual building where it all began, their historic caves, brew kettles, as well as a very impressive welcoming center. An exciting and informative tour (along with free samples!) guarantees a memory few forget.

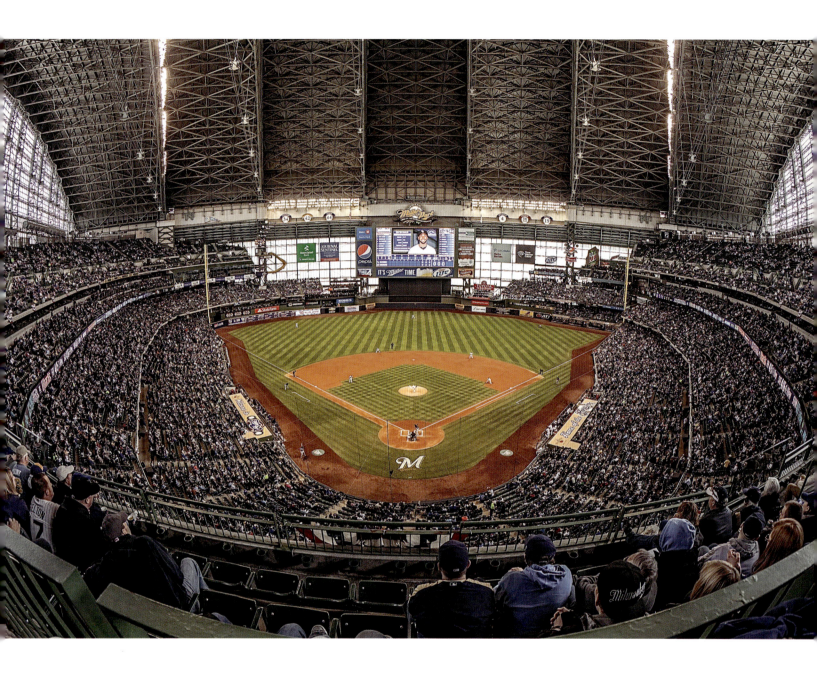

Miller Park

On your way back to the Pfister you'll most likely spot the imposing Miller Park and its retractable roof. It's home to the beloved Milwaukee Brewers Baseball Club. In addition, Miller Park has hosted some of the most spectacular concerts in the country.

BMO Harris Bradley Center

One major sport not enough for you? Consider that just about ten blocks away from the Pfister is the BMO Harris Bradley Center where the Milwaukee Bucks of the NBA take on the competition. The Center is also home to Marquette University basketball, the Milwaukee Admirals hockey team, and it hosts some of the greatest entertainment names and productions the world has to offer.

Pabst Theater

For more music, drama, comedy, musicals, magic and other spectacular theatrics, the Pfister is near two of the world's finest such venues. The Pabst Theater and Marcus Center for the Performing Arts.

The "Pabst" as it is commonly known, is an historic masterpiece built around the same time as the Pfister. Seating over 1,300, it was designed in an opulent German Renaissance Revival style, and its stage has seen the likes of Tchaikovsky, Rachmaninoff, Olivier and Pavlova, to name a few. These days it hosts a wide array of entertainment that tends to thrive in a classical, unique, and intimate environment.

Marcus Center for the Performing Arts

Just a block away is Milwaukee's most popular and well-known performance venue: Marcus Center for the Performing Arts—home of the Milwaukee Symphony Orchestra, Milwaukee Ballet, City Ballet Theater, First Stage Children's Theater, and the Florentine Opera, among others. Since opening its door in 1969, it has hosted a virtual who's-who of stars, luminaries, Broadway musicals, actors, and soloists from every corner on Earth. This world-class, state-of-the-art facility boasts multiple performance spaces, an outdoor concert pavilion, large and small banquet rooms, meeting rooms, lecture halls and lounge accommodations, plus on-site catering. In short, a seemingly entire city of arts and culture all under one amazing roof.

Summerfest

And then there's the Fest that made Milwaukee Famous: The Big Gig! Summerfest!!

Widely recognized as the "World's Largest Music Festival," it attracts over seven hundred bands and acts, hundreds of thousands of spectators, and runs for eleven days in late June/early July. Located inside the Henry W. Maier Festival Park, it's sprawled along the beautiful shores of Lake Michigan, and just a hop, skip and a jump from the Pfister. Summerfest is far more than an eleven stage music venue. The grounds feature an enormous and varied selection of delicious foods and beverages, shopping vendors, children's and family activities, and arguably some of the most breathtaking fireworks displays enjoyed anywhere.

The crowning glory of the enormous festival park is the Marcus Amphitheater.

Nestled at the south end of the grounds, right on the shoreline, stands this state-of-the-art, 25,000 mostly covered seat-capacity performance experience.

In addition to Summerfest, the festival park plays host to a long list of other fairs, fests and concerts, including Pridefest, Polish Fest, Festa Italiana, German Fest, African World Festival, Irish Fest, Mexican Fiesta and Indian Summer Festival.

ACKNOWLEDGMENTS

The pleasures of creating a book such as this come not merely from the Pfister's stunning environment, its timeless beauty and its hospitable personality, but from the remarkable people who we've had the good fortune to encounter along the way. And those who have graced her halls before any of us.

We would genuinely like to thank *Ben Marcus*, the visionary who saw this fine hotel as a dusty diamond and believed in its unending charm and potential for becoming and remaining world-class, welcoming guests from every walk-of-life.

Steve Marcus, the carrier of the torch from his father Ben, and the dreamer who dedicated himself to creating and maintaining a standard of excellence unrivaled anywhere. Many of the design, comfort and artistic embellishments over the decades were of his vision and under his stewardship. And of course, *Greg Marcus*, the present day "keeper-of-the-keys." Greg is now the ardent proprietor responsible for maintaining the age-old integrity, the uncompromising level of services, the future developments, innovations and enhancements. Plus, some brilliant hotel, dining and entertainment concepts, like the popular Mason Street Grill. In short, the modern day innkeeper whose passion revolves around the complete care and aesthetics of the Pfister's heart and soul, not to mention its precious contents and its cherished visitors.

This book was the brainchild of Marcus Corporation's *Chris W. Anderson*, an energetic pacesetter who oversees all marketing, sales, and brand development for all US hotel properties in the company's portfolio. He continually championed this book's progress and supported, encouraged and piloted us throughout the development of its contents.

Many, many thanks to *Joe Kurth, Omar Naimi, Peggy Williams-Smith, Stephan Fitz, Greg Owens, Rosie DeRubertis, Christopher Kanzelberger, Ed Carella,* and *Cassy Scrima*. Each one a valued member of the Pfister family, and each one generous and accommodating with their time, insights, their hotel information, their experiences, memories and stories. A universal love of their jobs and genuine appreciation for their place of work was evident everyday of our visits.

Chefs *Brian Frakes, Mark Weber* and *Jennifer Carlson*, top-of-their-game professionals with crazy, busy schedules, each found time for us.

In addition contributions of time and input were gladly given by *Rosemary Steinfest, Rocman Whitesell, Annie Fang, Juan Rodriguez, Blake Lawrence, Donna Basterash, Bradley Wooten,* and *Michael Wesner*.

But our most treasured alliances were with a pair of the Pfister's finest, *Michelle McGarragher* and *Peter Mortensen*.

Michelle's dedication to the Pfister is likely unmatched. Excelling as a masterful juggler and composed manager of everyday details, staff, guest, event, and celebrity concerns, right down to this nook and that cranny. Her organizational skills, combined with her lovely personality, made her positively invaluable to us.

And Peter, Concierge par excellence, is he. No one knows more about this magnificent building than Peter. No one. And nobody dotes on its legacy and its importance as he does. Few people know Milwaukee better than Peter Mortensen. He is the sagest of historians. He is the epitome of charm. His unabashed love of the Pfister could be considered a force unto itself. Peter is the beloved ambassadorial conduit of the Pfister's magnificent past and its bright future. He is known and respected by countless guests and luminaries.

On the creative side we had wonderful assistance from some outstanding local professionals, including *Nick Collura* of Collura Creative, *Debra Zindler* and *Cory Zimmermann* of Z2 Marketing, *Jim McDonald* of Laughlin/Constable. Artists *Cathy Prtizl, Gina Ferrise* and *Gary Bakic*. *Sarah Hopley* of Milwaukee County Historical Society. The Milwaukee Public Library Main Branch; *Leslie Heinrichs,* and *Paul C. Weise*.

THOMAS J. JORDAN

Tom Jordan is an international award-winning advertising writer and the former Chairman and Chief Creative Officer of Hoffman York Advertising. He is also the author of four top-selling books on marketing. Tom includes music among his many passions and has written over a dozen original songs, one of which was recorded by Ray Charles. Tom now lives in Door County with his wife Susan, where he continues his work on book projects.

authorthomasjordan.com

JAY W. FILTER

Creative Director Jay Filter spent the thirty plus years of his award-winning advertising career hiring dozens of photographers to fulfill his visions. A few years back he took to the craft himself to enhance his extensive travels. Once his clients began to recognize his skills, a second career path came into existence. Now, instead of receiving accolades for his writing and design, he graciously accepts citations for shooting beautiful pictures.

jayfilterphotography.com

STEVE BIEL

Multi-talented designer/art director Steve Biel's diverse and accredited experience, in both print and web-based projects, has spanned high-level positions at the Minnesota Orchestra and *Minnesota Monthly* publications as well as having served as Director of Design and Publications at the renown Milwaukee Art Museum. When he's not at his computer he's usually found in his garden or out and active amongst nature, where he likes to say his dog takes *him* for a walk! Steve now works independently for a wide-ranging array of clients.

stevebiel.com

PICTURE NOTES

Page numbers in bold

5, Rosette flourish, main staircase

6-7, Carving from lobby fireplace

8-9, Rhapsodies in Blu

10-11, Ornate faces, main lobby

12-13, Floral settee

14-15, Phoebe, goddess of intellect

18-19, Magnificent swan faucet

20-21, Decorative french period piece

22-23, Left: whimsical rope twist leg Right: Our beautiful fabric pattern

24-25, Clockwise from upper left: Charles Pfister, original key and room number fob, vintage color shot of original lobby layout, party panoramic photo, early century dining menu, group shot of the Pfister's chefs from 1930. Top of right-hand page: one of the hotel's stunning chandeliers.

28-29, Looking south on Jefferson

30-31, Looking northeast from the former main post office, now the Federal Courthouse

34-35, The breathtaking lobby as you walk through the main doors

36-37, Old fashioned-style, working phone along second floor hallway

38-39, Beautifully detailed door handles and lock plates

40-41, Sunburst mirror on left, one of the original door knockers on right

52, Main lobby looking south

60-61, Pfister's posh, comfy lounge

62-63, Holiday festooning

64-65, World-class ceiling mural in main lobby

70-71, Elaborate staircase finials

78-79, Serene relaxation area

80-81, Former outdoor balcony entrance, now a guest room

82-83, Second floor looking southwest

86, Well Spa reception seating

92-93, Highlights of Pfister's Well Spa and Salon

94-95, Do Not Disturb Spa fob

96-97, Signature guest robes

96-97, Spa refreshments

102-103, Well Spa elements

104-105, Well Spa elements

106-107, Well Spa Salon

118-119, Imperial Ballroom decked out for fashion event

120-121, Imperial Ballroom chandelier on left, Grand Ballroom on right

122-123, Posh reception area, center of seventh floor event rooms

124-125, Close-up of one of the brilliant chandeliers of the Pfister

126-127, Imperial Ballroom dais on left, balcony view of the Imperial on right

128-129, Readying for the festivities

130-131, Cafe Rouge all decked out

132-133, Imperial Ballroom awaiting the Bridal party and guests

140-141, Mason Street Grill's stunning main dining room

142-143, Mason Street Grill's counter side

144-145, Mason Street Grill glassware

146-147, Mason Street Grill's plush seating on left, bar on right

148-149, Mason Street Grill, classy and casual

150-151, Counter side

152-153, Mason Street Grill close-ups

154-155, Awaiting the big chill

156-157, Mason Street Grill bar area

160-161, Your table awaits you in Blu

162-163, Pull up a chair and relax in Blu

164-165, Fine wine glasses

166-167, Inspiration for the name Blu

172-173, Classic design and comfort

174-175, Various room highlights

176-177, Beckoning comfort

178-179, Classic Pfister room design and comfort

180-181, More room perfection

182-183, Sleek, sophisticated comfort

184-185, Unwind, relax, have a seat

186-187, Sleek designs in every room

188-189, Suite design and aesthetics

190-191, Sunrise from the tower

192-219, The art and imagery of the Pfister Hotel

220-250, The smiling, happy members of the Pfister Family

252-267, Featuring selected artworks from the Pfister Hotel's art collection

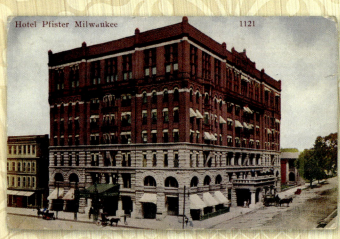